M000012587

THE NATIONAL POETRY SERIES

The National Poetry Series was established in 1978 to ensure the
publication of five poetry books annually through five participating
publishers. Publication is funded annually by the Lannan Foundation,
Stephen Graham, Juliet Lea Hillman Simonds, and The Poetry
Foundation. For a complete listing of generous contributors to
The National Poetry Series, please visit www.nationalpoetryseries.org.

2013 Competition Winners

Ampersand Revisited
by Simeon Berry of Somerville, Massachusetts
Chosen by Ariana Reines, to be published by Fence Books

Trespass
by Thomas Dooley of New York, New York
Chosen by Charlie Smith, to be published by HarperCollins Publishers

Bone Map
by Sara Eliza Johnson of Salt Lake City, Utah
Chosen by Martha Collins, to be published by Milkweed Editions

Its Day Being Gone
by Rose McLarney of Tulsa, Oklahoma
Chosen by Robert Wrigley, to be published by Penguin Books

What Ridiculous Things We Could Ask of Each Other
by Jeffrey Schultz of Los Angeles, California
Chosen by Kevin Young, to be published by University of Georgia Press

WHAT
RIDICULOUS
THINGS WE
COULD ASK
OF EACH
OTHER

What Ridiculous Things We Could Ask of Each Other

POEMS BY JEFFREY SCHULTZ

The University of Georgia Press ∴ Athens and London

© 2014 by the University of Georgia Press
Athens, Georgia 30602
www.ugapress.org
All rights reserved
Designed by Erin Kirk New
Set in 10.2 on 15 Garamond Premier Pro
Printed and bound by Sheridan Books
The paper in this book meets the guidelines for
permanence and durability of the Committee on
Production Guidelines for Book Longevity of the
Council on Library Resources.

Most University of Georgia Press titles are
available from popular e-book vendors.

Printed in the United States of America

18 17 16 15 14 P 5 4 3 2 1

Library of Congress Cataloging-in-Publication Data
Schultz, Jeffrey, 1979–
   [Poems. Selections]
   What ridiculous things we could ask of each other : poems /
by Jeffrey Schultz.
      pages cm. — (The national poetry series)
   ISBN 978-0-8203-4721-9 (pbk. : alk. paper) — ISBN 0-8203-4721-3
(pbk. : alk. paper)
   I. Title.
   PS3619.C47823A6   2014
   811'.6—dc23   2014002336

British Library Cataloging-in-Publication Data available

Contents

What Ridiculous Things We Could Ask of Each Other

Acknowledgments

Thanks to the editors and staffs of the following publications, in which some of the poems from this collection originally appeared, sometimes in slightly different form:

32 Poems: "The Soul as Rooms for Rent"

Anti-: "Inner City Circular Saw Cosmology Blues" and "The Soul as a Kind of Life I Sort of Lived Once"

Boston Review: "J. Steals from the Rich and Uses the Money to Get Drunk Again"

Boxcar Poetry Review: "The Soul as Social Service Caseworker"

Copper Nickel: "The Soul as Episode in the Supermarket" and "The Soul as Kaczynski"

Great River Review: "Power Outage, Fresno, California, August 10, 1996"

Grist: "As If Someone Were Trying to Tell Us Something"

Indiana Review: "Old News and the Borrowed Blues"

Linebreak: "Our Lady of the Electrical Substation"

Miramar: "To the Unexploded H-Bomb Lost in Tidal Mud off the Coast of Savannah, Georgia" and "J. Listens to Line Static on the Last Pay Phone in the Continental U.S."

Missouri Review: "J. Resists the Urge to Comment on Your Blog" and "The Gathering Blues"

Northwest Review: "These Arms of Mine"

PBS NewsHour's Art Beat Online: "J. Begins by Saying *The World's Not as It Should Be*"

Poetry: "J. Learns the Difference between Poverty and Having No Money" and "J. Finds in His Pocket Neither Change nor Small Bills"

Poetry Northwest: "Weekday Apocalyptic"

Prairie Schooner: "The Mourner's Fare" and "Permanent Collection"

Solo Cafe: "The Day before the Revolution"
Solo Novo: "Apocalypse When?"

"J. Steals from the Rich and Uses the Money to Get Drunk Again" and
"The Soul as Kaczynski" have been featured on *Poetry Daily*; "J. Learns the
Difference between Poverty and Having No Money" has been anthologized
in *Poets of the American West*; *Poem of the Week* featured "J. Learns the
Difference between Poverty and Having No Money" and "J. Finds in
His Pocket Neither Change nor Small Bills"; "Weekday Apocalyptic"
and "J. Finds in His Pocket Neither Change nor Small Bills" have been
anthologized in *Apocalypse Now: Poems and Prose from the End of Days*.

Thanks to the Poetry Foundation, which through a Ruth Lilly
Fellowship provided generous financial support that made the completion
of this manuscript possible.

Thanks to Kevin Young, Stephanie Stio, and the National Poetry
Series, and to Sydney DuPre, Jon Davies, and everyone at the University of
Georgia Press.

Thanks to my family, to Chuck and Dianne Hanzlicek, to Peter
Everwine, Connie Hales, Dorianne Laux, and Pimone Triplett. Thanks also
to Mark Looker, Neal Migan, Bob Campbell, and Megan Levad. Thanks
to Cyndy Holder and to Allison Perkins. Special thanks to Garrett Hongo
and Joshua Robbins, to whom these poems owe so much.

Most especially, thanks to Leah Hanzlicek, without whom I would have
never either written a poem in the first place or, in the fullest possible sense,
known poetry.

WHAT
RIDICULOUS
THINGS WE
COULD ASK
OF EACH
OTHER

J. Begins by Saying *The World's Not as It Should Be*

And then, embarrassed at the conversation's sudden death,
    all eyes at once on him, and daunted, honestly, at the prospect
Of going on, of cataloging, in detail, the slow distension
    each child's belly must endure, and each piece of flesh
Cauterized without knowing it would be, without any time
    to prepare before the glowing hot shrapnel enters it
And passes through—not, certainly, that preparation
    would help in any way—he raises his glass back to his lips
And listens to the others go on as before, listens as the bar noise swells,
    exile's new fashion for the season, softer, sure, but harder, perhaps,
From which to find one's way back. Even at the get-go, it was stupid,
    the idea he could make such a list, and that, once made,
It might be useful for some thing or other. No. It's idle chit-
    chat, gossip: . . . *said what . . . . . . always has been a bitch . . .* ,
And the jukebox's brief pause between two more three-minute
    spins through nothingness. We join in. We sit out,
But, end of the night, there's hardly any difference as he scuffs
    up the leaf-scent on the cold walk home, the sky above crisp
With autumn's first deep chill. The last buses have run their routes,
    have ferried, in their blue fluorescence, the faces of the tired
To wherever it is the tired disappear. The streets are deserted.
    My friends, please forgive my prying, but what have you all
Been up to lately? I feel like we never talk anymore,
    like keeping in touch, for no good reason, has become
Impossible. Instead, long walks, bus rides, the self-checkout lane's
    smudged touch screen and hideously inoffensive *thank you*
For shopping, then too many drinks each evening and these half-read
    stacks of books' stillness as I fall asleep in spite of some

Sitcom's laugh-track, complication, one-liner, cheap resolution.

Tell me, have you been well? Where you are, wherever that is,
What colors, what scents does this time of year bring?

Under skies like this, we think distances might dissolve; I almost see
You there, your eyes barely able to track the words any longer, your hands
cold, always, for some reason, cold. It would have been nice
If we'd lived closer together. We could see each other sometimes,
not have to worry over someone to feed the cat, talk to him a little,
Water the plants, keep an eye on all these things. But that's it:
I can only imagine, and no better than I can imagine anything,
Which means, as I sit here looking out of your skull,
it's the frames of my own glasses at the blurred edge
Of our vision. My double, or yours? If yours, I like your taste
in whiskey. Friend, once I dreamed of a beautiful country,
And both of us were there, and everyone we do and do not know,
and I tell you, I miss that place. I wish I could say just
Where we should go. O, my country, my lost and human country.

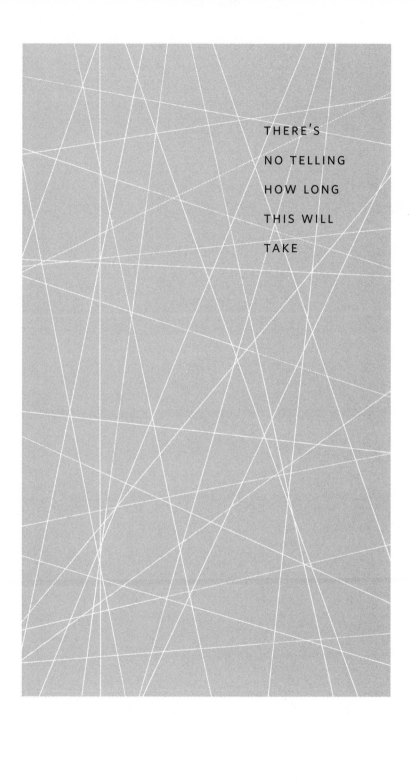

THERE'S
NO TELLING
HOW LONG
THIS WILL
TAKE

Our Lady of the Electrical Substation

He'd been a tourist in churches, there for a look at the glass
    and a half-hearted pang of the sublime beneath vaulted ceilings,

But there was always the flickering silhouette of some woman
    who prayed over a candle she'd lit; then the guilt

Of the faithless would usher him out to afternoon's heat-
    dazzled streets. After the corner store's worn linoleum

And six pack, he wondered if he could feel anything holy
    given years of the nightly news's nightly war, given

His wife's retelling of her days working with abused
    and molested children. So when he came across these

Beautiful, deadly coils risen up toward heaven and the power
    lines that converged in a perfect cage to hold it back,

He couldn't explain the current that ran through him,
    except to say the hum of it, the substation's carcinogenic

Psalm, seemed to cycle at the same rate as the soul,
    which stirred slightly from its hibernation

In the unpainted apse at the back of its hermetic cell.

Weekday Apocalyptic

Summer already, the bright edge of morning's blade slits
    through the fence boards and lays its blinding scar tissue
Across the dew-blacked and shadowed lawn. Every day
    seems more like this, the verge of extinction with coffee
And a roll on the back stoop. This is my breakfast, this, the air
    saturated with small-engine exhaust as the neighborhood's
Undocumented laborers get down to business, their hats
    pulled low on their brows to block the piercing eyes
Of young and terrified mothers who stroll around aimlessly,
    dreaming of something before, worrying over what's to come:
A whole future of PTA meetings and weathered clothespins
    which cast shadows like swallows' tails cut and clipped
For display. A flicker rattles off his SOS on a telephone pole.
    Inside, the kitchen radio's wilting out news from the front
And the world is bleeding out again in the tub; the darkening water
    cups her breasts as she slips in and out of consciousness.
She half-hears people leaving for work, dogs barking, sounds
    which blend then in her mind with the cries of amputee children.
They open wounds in her pastoral dreams the way police searchlights
    part the sacred dark. There's no telling how long this will take;
The cut's deep, but above the noise, you hear something in her choking:
    between shallow breaths and the warm water sloshing,
You can tell she doesn't want this; you can tell she's a fighter.

Power Outage, Fresno, California, August 10, 1996

One-hundred-fifteen degrees, and the grid's been knocked flat.
   All afternoon, stillness and a hush like I've never heard,

But now, as the sun sinks below thousands of tract homes'
   rooflines, as the space between shadows shifts

From bright whites to oranges and purples, as the heat
   stands down and slips its blade back into its belt,

A little *get you tomorrow, punk* in its swagger as it rounds the corner,
   the city rises up slowly, gravel gouged in its knees,

And thanks Jesus for the chance to choke in the ozone-thick air.
   Cooler, finally, outside than in, everyone's laid out broken

On the stoop with half-warmed beers or sun tea and what's left
   of the ice, or else they wander in dazed pairs on the older,

Tree-lined streets. There isn't a single siren or gunshot,
   not the rattle of a distant argument or an air conditioner's hum.

There's no traffic, and no subwoofer's bass line threatens
   to shake the world apart. After a collective beat-down,

There's an implicit truce, and this one could last all night.
   Everyone may as well be in love, though there's no way to know it;

You couldn't manage to pull together a single thought
   if you tried, so there's no way to look forward,

No way to look back. No way to know this girl by my side,
  around whose waist I've not yet even slipped my arm,

Will become the woman who will become my wife, no way
  to know life's blunt and endless hours of filing insurance forms

Or the sudden embarrassment of going absolutely blank
  in the middle of a produce aisle, artificial light buzzing

Above the plasticky lemons. As if heat had fused The Real
  and whatever lies just beyond its reach; as if we were subject

To both fate and that glowing possibility, that first blue
  arcing of current from one transformer to the next,

Of pure chance. It's absolutely everything charged into absolutely
  nothing more than the dulled, relentless fever

Of now, which presses so hard we can't help but feel filled.

As If Someone Were Trying to Tell Us Something

Summer's blast furnace could peel the skin
    right back from your face, and still the road-resurfacing crew
Pours their thinned, hot asphalt over the patchwork
    concrete and weeds of the street. All morning,

Through the growl of machinery, the scrape of tools,
    right-wing radio's pounding fist and static,
I've been trying to get the house in order,
    knowing the whole time it's no use:

Kitchen linoleum peeling, pine floors pitted and scarred.
    I can't even get through the dusting, so eager,
With each trinket I pick up from the shelf, to reconstruct
    the sheen of some history it might have had,

And I mean history beyond the scattered anecdotes
    and half-truths from which we patch our life together
So that we might tell it, someday, as if it were a story,
    a story, even, of some particular interest,

But I mean I want the smooth and cool and dustless surface
    of this green-glazed ceramic ashtray to speak
When I ask, to tell what rude or delicate hands
    shaped it with such practiced imperfection, to tell how,

After the end of a shift, those hands, sometimes pocketed
    and sometimes not, ached with the pain
Of repetitive motion on the long walk home, how the woman,
    if it was a woman, wondered at how she could pass

Through signs of life, wisps of cigarette smoke, phrases
      of music lost to the breeze, when no one at all was out
With her on those streets. And how the kiln would fire
      all through the night while she sat at the kitchenette's table

Lost in some colorless booze. I want the almost imperceptible
      web of cracks in the glaze to confess everything,
Down to the name of the politician who sits now, hair parted
      in a perfectly straight line which reveals his scalp,

In some sex club's neon-framed shadows. It's because
      he attached a rider quietly to some bill that no one
Bothered to read anyway that thousands of hands
      have been condemned to thousands of years of labor

Which are forgotten sooner than the sweat can evaporate
      from his upper lip and add its grease to this room's
Particular mist, while for the first time all week he jerks off
      no one but himself. Only there's no knowing

Which politician, which nondescript building,
      which gray industrial district in which featureless city,
Which tired hands and which harmless looking
      and vaguely worded line of law that translates

Into vernacular as *bow down*. With the details smoothed over,
      any truth's a lost cause, I'm thinking, as if we're built up
On nothing but a compacted bed of everything we don't know
      and can't hope to understand. Outside, the crew's smoothed

Over forty years of weather and wear by lunch time.
    They move off to another block; the smell of cancer,
The whole dark history of tar, hangs in the air,
    and as I stare at the anonymous destruction

Of this living room's floor, I can't help but wonder,
    with time, what will happen to us, the body broken
And the body sutured together again.
    And if we're lucky enough, you and I, to grow old,

I wonder what we might find, the whole weight
    of the unknown pulsing just beneath the surface.
I wonder, some evening, as we watch the night
    slap its coat of black across the sky, east to west,

Is to isn't, what that old breeze, as it passes over our thinning,
    almost translucent skin and chills the untraceable
Blue web of veins gathered there, might be willing to confess
    about where it's been and where we all must be heading.

J. Learns the Difference between Poverty and Having No Money

after Ernesto Trejo

And the morning's marine layer cloud cover's just beginning to unhinge,
    to let the buttery light of another daybreak slip through
And weigh down the dead lawns and sagging rooftops
    of this neighborhood, where Cold War–era television antennas
Still cast shadows like B-52s heading offshore, where poverty, this early
    is the smell of Malt-O-Meal and the dregs of thin beer
Washed down the sink. Where the shift begins at 7 AM,
    but consciousness has a way of coming round as slowly
As this old computer monitor flickers its dull sixteen colors into being.
    On it, the names and numbers of laundromat and liquor store owners,
Fast-food managers and lawn-care companies; it's my job
    to cold-call them, read from a script on the benefits of membership
In the Executive Dining Club, not take *No* for an answer.
    I'm no good and both the boss and I know it, and he's hovering
When the scraped-out voice of the woman on my phone answers me with
    My husband's been killed, and then, instead of hanging up,
Throws the receiver down next to something—dishwasher or window AC,
    I don't know—but something close, it sounds, to tearing itself apart,
Something cycling through an awful, screeching noise.
    And it's because I've paused that the boss flings a pencil
Into the wall in front of me and edges closer, and because of the fear
    of unemployment forms or the sky opening up if I were to walk out,
And because this sound—the un-oiled, flak-fouled crack of it—
    has left me standing suddenly at the end of a runway, where planes
Scream low overhead, loaded for the beginning of the end of the world,
    that I start back into the script, start back as if I believe each word,
Even though, in the rattle and dust of the jet-wash, no one hears a thing.

The Soul as Social Service Caseworker

The two-way-mirrored visitation room's empty at last,
    and she's beat. A full hour the Liver and the Will argued,

Unwilling each to understand the other's point of view.
    Swollen and belligerent, the Liver demands sole

Custody; the Will, little brat, has counterpetitioned
    for emancipation. It goes nowhere. It seems always

To go nowhere. Outside, the office-park's parking lot's
    nearly empty in the dusty early evening;

Only a never-once-washed early model Volvo
    and a Toyota Tercel wagon remain. They seem,

In fact, to have been abandoned, their once good-hearted
    owners having vanished as so many before into the archives

In search of the one case history which would illuminate
    all others. Sometimes they're found wandering bile ducts,

Dazed; sometimes not. Only Memory, a department decimated
    by budget cuts, has a backlog deeper than hers, but she's trying

To dig out, puts in a few more hours off the clock: referrals
    for alcohol, depression, debt management, job training.

Everything in triplicate. Everything in a sort of untrained
    legalese. When she finally nods off, head propped

On a stack of forms, she dreams in the problems
    of others, dreams in paper cut and file folders' endless

Beige. They're stacked so high, you can't even see
    the cubicle walls, which are covered in clipped

Comics, print-outs of funny email forwards, kids' painted
    pictures, the small things that make life at all bearable.

The Day before the Revolution

His songs sounded new enough by name,
    "The City's a Blast Crater" and "Car Bomb Blues,"
But they weren't the kind of thing anyone

    wanted to hear anymore: sparse twelve-bar
On piano and the shock, here and there, of harmonica
    amplified like a bomber passing overhead,

Petroleum's sudden, unexpected smell then,
    just before the napalm lights. Besides,
He always played just a tick behind the beat, a little

    out of time, just as all the greats had,
Just as no one did anymore; people, after all,
    had schedules to keep. He bussed tables

In a café in one of the new part of town's
    sprawling strip malls stuccoed and styled
To evoke in those who'd never been to one a buzzing

    Mediterranean piazza. The hill on which it sat
Overlooked the old city center, and patrons, on rare days
    when the smog would yield a view,

Would try to spot signs of life. *How can anyone
    survive down there,* they would ask,
Offering punctuation in the disinterested *clink*

of another olive's pit spit into a plate
Which served no other purpose. After months of begging
    the boss to let him play, *blacklisted*

Is what he decided to call it and so quit without thinking
    of money, of food or rent, of the inevitable,
Which, in the language he knew best,

    was eviction and nowhere left to go.
And so a garage sale and, one morning,
    a borrowed Chevy pickup to move the rest

Back to his mother's. Its shocks creaked out the sound
    of his failure as he slid his ancient upright
From the porch across some planks

    and into the truck's bed. Then the filthy street's
Yellow light caught up on the dust-caked windshield
    and the song he was writing in his head,

"The Day before the Revolution," as he jerked
    this way and that through the holy chaos
Of downtown's morning traffic, a sudden lurch, then,

    around a bus and the piano gone clear
Over the bed's edge and into an empty crosswalk,
    the crash of it every individual thing

That ever touched those keys at once:
    piano tuner's pure and repeated elation
At a pure and accurate tone, love songs,

impromptu and always in the key of C,
The endless, unnuanced contempt of a girl forced
every night for years to practice her Bach,

The purposeful errors to spite her parents,
and her joy, wholly unexpected, the night her hands
Began to move as if independent of her mind,

every pound of tension on every inch of string,
Every silent year in every widower's living room,
every note beyond every scale's end,

All of it rang suddenly against the asphalt
and the world stopped: the wind and the ticket stubs
Blowing in it, day laborers waiting for work,

bus riders, sidewalk prophets and the splintered sect
Of black-clad and ascetic back-alley prophets,
tattooed punks and wandering pensioners,

Even the vendors of nothing itself stopped,
turned their heads and began to gather, to look,
To listen to this sound they'd never heard before

but which felt inevitable as the explosion's crack
And ball of flame when the timer's ticked down past zero,
a thing they'd always known but never dared imagine,

A thing that wouldn't stop ringing in their ears.

Parable of the Blind Man

Young, he'd look at the sun long as he could stand
    before turning away and clamping down his eyelids.
He'd then try to decipher the blurred pictographs, messages,

    he was certain, his soul had etched into the capillaries.
Nothing much came of it, except, decades later,
    macular degeneration and a fleet of cataracts

Which ferried all his sight to the thick waters of a vision.
    Now, guided by the arm of his exhausted eldest daughter
Up and down the aisles of the discount supermarket,

    we might be anyone to him: dead wife or dead lover,
Dead siblings or friends. We are indistinct, muted nothingness
    wandering a maze of bulk-bins and off-brand canned goods;

We are the cold currents of the freezer section who line up
    willingly to be checked out and swept away in a river
Of the featureless, our good works and sins washed clean.

WITHOUT OUR EVEN

KNOWING IT

The Gathering Blues

⠂⠄

Here is the blueness of dawn-break and the blueness
    of moon-glow framing the cold above snow.

Here, suddenly a single phrase of song half-recognized,
    and in its wake, a silence like settled dust.

Here is the bright spine of each log behind the stove's glass
    revealed, then crumbling into a whiteness blinding

As the light of day again out of the lobby after the matinee.
    We've all known the pain of not knowing,

The black stars in our eyes, their meaningless constellations,
    as we stand there on the street, as our pupils clamp down

And the story we've lived for the last hour and a half fades
    suddenly back to the details of our own lives.

The street's filthy slush and the buses' tires slipping through it.
    Our afternoon's emptiness, which has left us here,

Cold hands pocketed outside the downtown's only theater,
    the tint of the overcast's shadowless light

Bluing the neglected marquee, which tells us nothing
    about what to do next.

⠂⠄

∵

We are the dawn-break and its blueness holds
    on all day sometimes and into the night.

And we know—we've seen enough movies to know—
    that as long as this art-film light holds out

Nothing is going to happen. So we do what we've always done:
    dust and rearrange the framed photos and small stones

We've picked up over the years; use them to build little altars
    to our pasts on mantles and windowsills,

The tops of our televisions, so we'll see them sometimes
    when the plot gets thin. As it has now, as we step out

Into the snow-bound street for a break in the clouds,
    try to guess what it is the few stars have to tell us

About our lives, try to shake this suspicion that God's
    fallen asleep in the projection booth, the loose end

Of the reel flapping and His chin rested in the crook
    of His arm as He dreams a different Creation.

∵

∴

We are walking with nowhere to go, and the songs we hum,
    the songs we love and can't quite remember,

We are those too. The same few notes repeating
    without resolution, until, without our even knowing it,

They shift into something else, something almost
    unrecognizable, Orion's arm and the body obscured

By clouds. Here, nothing's ever clear; nothing's ever finished,
    and in the dim light of the parties we sometimes

Find ourselves in the midst of, our stories always suffer for it,
    trail off and end in the awkward

Clinking of ice cubes, or fingers tapping the bottom of a glass
    to the tune of the scratched 78's blues on the stereo.

And still the hostess makes the rounds, makes sure
    everyone mingles in the risen dust her dusting earlier

Has left suspended in the air. Each one of us breathes it in.
    Each one of us swipes our hands through it

To emphasize some point we want to make.
    And in our motion's wake, the dust gathers again,

As if, somehow, we already spoke with the gestures of the dead.

∴

∴

And so it should come as no surprise, when sometimes we stare
    at our hands, numb and blued in the cold, and have trouble

Recognizing them as our own. These knuckles dark
    and each scar outlined in white seem to tell stories

Beyond what we've known, stories that begin and end gathered
    around a fire, stories of prayer and song, the palms

Of an entire people open to the ancient moon's living glow.
    These hands have endured, we think; these hands

Have been brave, though we only know bravery as it's told
    in war movies and old newsreels, the shell's screech

And impact, the bit players' corpses obscured by soil
    and razor wire, the camera still moving after death.

And not a word of what the brave must pass into.

∴

∵

And what if we could bear to look straight into it,
　　and the future's fade-to-white only passed us,

With no more revelation than a car in the oncoming lane?
　　The trails its headlamps left in our eyes, how we had to try

To not steer into the blankness. Then the moon-glow
　　on the snow and the vineyards' withered canes disappearing

In snow on either side of the highway until there was nothing
　　but the road. As if Creation itself had contempt

For its endless details and only wanted to show us, for once,
　　the way, same as this kid whose pitted face

Burns behind the box-office glass when we ask for one
　　to some movie even we know we shouldn't

Waste our time with. He dreams all day of denying
　　us admittance to it. He wants everyone to see only

What's meaningful. But we only want to see something happen.
　　Or at least feel something's about to happen,

To be brought to the brink before the record skips back
　　over the last phrase again, needle fouled with dust.

∵

∵

And we shouldn't be too sad at the thought of dust gathering
    and no one to wipe it away or scatter it even with a breath

Or the breeze of a body passing through a room, because
    though no story is ever finished, they all, even,

Dear Ones, our own, must end. Though there's no reason,
    having come this far, we shouldn't linger

A little outside this theater, where it's dark now and snowing.
    Remember, even though we get the words wrong,

And the melody, beneath every song we sing is the blues,
    and everyone can count the blues, like it or not.

So count on it to rise up in you, when there's nothing else
    to count on, when the snow streaking

Through the marquee light may as well be tracer-fire,
    or streamers at some forgotten parade,

Or the TV reception gone out again and the entire zodiac
    come crashing down in the street.

Whatever it is, at some point you've just got to step out into it.

∵

WHEN YOU

HOLD AT LAST

THE MAGNIFIER

ABOVE THE

PAGE

Early Service at the Temple of Angelino Heights

Police helicopters' searchlights suddenly useless,
    dawn-break dispenses its smog-tinged grace on the pursued.

Kneeling, they catch their breath beneath dust-covered awnings
    of vacant shops and *mercados* before stepping back out

Into wide, concrete avenues and the anonymous multitudes
    we've all become. Some of us still sleep; some lament

Stale *pan dulce* and slug back burnt coffee, the very taste
    of exhaustion, on this hill above the pit from which the city

Has risen, but the true prophets have already taken to the streets;
    robed in sleek black Hondas, their glasspacks' snarl

And subwoofers' deep rumblings prepare the uninitiated
    for the tremors of this world's end. And though the curbside's

Deserted, each arched doorway echoes in strident rejoicing
    as an entire congregation of car alarms, with a pure and truly

Atrophied passion, ring out their hymn in a round.

The Soul as a Kind of Life I Sort of Lived Once

Some Final Four's glorious pick-and-roll rendered
    graceless and obscure by rabbit ears' static,

It's hard to focus on much anything of those days:
    scotch and popcorn maybe, whatever happened

To be around. Look at the way he shifts in the worn recliner,
    half-distracted by fifty years of lead-based

Brushstrokes over plaster and lath or the upholstery's
    tacky late-80s motif: on black background

Wandering pastel lines which curve, dissolve
    to scattered points, dim constellations, the gravity

Of which his eye can neither escape nor interpret
    as representative of anything but a mercifully passed

Fashion. Look at the way he's beginning to forget
    he once believed this would all lead to epiphany

Or revelation. Maybe not God himself hidden
    in a pattern, sure, but something at least. Just look

At him. Two showers a day sometimes. Paint
    comes down from the ceiling in sheets.

The Mourner's Fare

The mourner's fare is half-off and minus this miniature bourbon
　　for which the flight attendant refused to let me pay.

An hour yet to go from one dark, wet city to another
　　and a black and white photocopy of a death certificate

On thin paper in my jacket's breast pocket, and I'm done.
　　Done talking, done listening, and done with the man

In the seat next to me, who has covered, in detail,
　　his biography—Kansas to California, wife, divorce,

A job I couldn't make any sense of—up to present
　　and now, of all things, won't stop talking about Jesus.

After everything, I haven't the heart, or the spine,
　　or whatever it would take to tell him the moonless black

Screaming past the window and the rattle of ice
　　in a plastic cup is the only sermon worth listening to

Here in pew 25A, where the reading light's off
　　and someone's swapped the hymnal for a copy of SkyMall.

And just when he's getting to the part about my sins,
　　paid for in advance, he says, a synthesized bell

And a voice chime in from the overhead panel,
　　warn us things are about to get rough not two seconds

Before what feels like a straight eight-story drop, Coke cans
    and little offerings of pretzels scattered everywhere.

And then it takes a moment to realize that this man
    has clamped his pale hand down onto my own,

That he is not letting go, that his breath, everyone's breath,
    is held, suddenly, in anticipation of that final, sheer descent,

Its chorus of emergency buzzers and the miraculous
    appearance of a flimsy sacrament in the shape

Of a yellow plastic oxygen mask no one has any faith in.
    In the end we all exhale; in the end

It's nothing, a little more turbulence and the senses returning.
    In the end the man up front, benevolent always,

Carries us through, though we've not a single thing
    left to our names, save the cargo of our own precious lives.

First Time around the Floor

What was it I wanted to say? *Sky pale blue as a robin's egg*
  or *this robin egg, pale blue and thin as the sky*?
And what would it matter here, dark back booth

  of another bar, happy hour still a distant dream
And early afternoon's washed-out light blistered
  by the front window's neon? Why was it

I came here: sullen shadows and the cold clack
  of billiard balls? God knows I'm too old for this.
It's not that we fight exactly, but every argument

  leaves us shut up and terrified like young lovers
Waiting on a home pregnancy test. One line or two?
  Red line or blue? The only thing certain's

That no one will speak, no matter what there is to say.
  It's that old pull again: when nothing much matters,
Nothing much lasts. Sky and the robin? Robin and sky?

  Look, I've got enough change for two songs on the jukebox
And a little time still before I've got to head home.
  I'm thinking "Pale Blue Eyes" and "Lonely Teardrops,"

Something slow, something fast, what do you say?
  O, Emptiness; O, Void, take me one last time in your arms,
Won't you? Look at this thin and shimmering light.

  No more sulking. Teach me how to dance.

Old News and the Borrowed Blues

I'll play it and tell you what it is later.
MILES DAVIS

All winter the dog's run his track around the yard's edge
 deeper into the mud; he's pissed on the same fence-posts,

Snorted at the squirrel between the weathered boards,
 and he circles always, as if there were a better place to shit.

I don't think he has it in him to mind, but thing is, I can't stop
 feeling sorry for myself and the piss-poor state of my days:

Rain and a walk to the market. Rain and the same old news,
 the anchor trying to manage a segue from *seventeen burnt bodies*

To *ten tips to kick your shopping addiction* with something like grace.
 And there are forms to fill out and copays to make.

There's the institutional AC's unwavering rumble and hiss.
 But isn't that the thing about the blues? At bottom,

It's always the same: One, Four, Five, One, repeat. You always know
 what's coming, and only The Greats can make you forget

To expect it: we sleep in on weekends, eat breakfast late,
 sit at the kitchen table and listen to the radio.

But it's the waking I like best, whole hours of it, tangling
 and untangling our bodies, fixing on the grace of the neck

Or wrist before circling back into a dream of a day beginning.
   It used to nag at me—I was such a child—always asking,

Is this all there is? But these days together, a little sunlight
   out the window rinsing the leaf-tips of the familiar,

I tell you, Honey, we're the richest dogs on Earth.

The Velvet Underground's "Sweet Jane," from Two Minutes, Thirty-Three Seconds to Two Minutes, Fifty-One Seconds

Late spring's early heat already intolerable as the work
    we're each buried beneath, it's high-school hooky grown up
For us: we slip out of work and into the bar before noon
    where the jukebox is all ours and the day staff pour
With great generosity up to and above the glasses' rims until,
    sun-struck, half-drunk, we're out again: uneven WPA sidewalks
Where the day's undone another button on her blouse,
    and like the curve of the streets in these neighborhoods
In which we cannot afford to live, it's the curving line
    of her breast we walk up to its end: a hilltop, this city's
Last blooming and soon-to-wilt lilacs, your favorite,
    which means stopping every sixth second, leaning
Till you almost fall, sun-drunk, half-slumped in my arms
    when I catch you, which means this tugging at my sleeve
And your speech rising almost into song, which means I know
    I should shut up, not try to put a few words to it,
This thing, or even a tune. It's like good Lou said, *All the poets,*
    they studied rules of verse, and those ladies, they rolled their eyes,
But baby, you know I love those eyes. *Just watch me now*:

        Again some filing cabinet's clank as forms
        Are pulled, are sifted through, are filed. And glints
        Of newly gray along the temple. Bent,
        I'm sore from sweeping, laundry, other chores,
        But when to clean the countertops, the floors,
        The windows' dusty sills, those fingerprints
        So lightly pressed upon the glass, faint hints
        Of longing, all we hint at anymore—

O give us longer, All That Is Not Scheme,
Not Plan: outside, and suddenly we find
Mid-afternoon's way lost; our senses have fled
These sun-soaked streets where we've not ever been.
But when we find our way home? Never mind
The housework, girl, we're jumping into bed.

These Arms of Mine

after Otis Redding

The recent past a ring of empty tall boys and the near future
 summer's sweet evening music—hedge clippers and go-carts,
Cicada-buzz and children's distant squeals—, I twisted,
 on the far end of our long walk home, my ankle landing
A short and joyous leap from the bar's garden ledge

 to the sidewalk. Honey, you took my arm over your shoulder
And helped me, cursing, the rest of the way. Anymore,
 it takes fresh injury to get my mind off the regular
Pains. I'd like to tell you something sweet, that the smoldering
 ache that's taken up in my knee, in my lower back,

Burns off entirely when I hold you, but I'm trying to lie
 less these days. And does that mean I ought to offer up
The uglier truths, the fact, for instance, that more and more
 any given wince or writhe in bed may not be pleasure but strands
Of muscle pulled over-taut and snapped like guitar strings?

 On the stereo, Isaac Brock's just managing to get the words out:
The good times are killing me. Everyone I love sings
 with the strain of the defeated, and Otis is their king.
Leg elevated, reading liner notes on the living room couch,
 I can't help but notice these arms of mine. Already, the skin's

Falling away from the muscle underneath, and I can't keep track
      which of the past's idiocies are marked by which scars.
A rough descent from some chain-link or slivered glass? Dog's tooth
      or the hard crash on cold gravel after leaping from a train?
It's a wonder I'm alive, but let's face it, I'm a mess. And in the far-off

      future, light angles, lemon, through someday's window
And spreads across the bedsheets. Outside, the sky's pale blue
      and thin as a robin's egg, and the bees work on the last
Of the hydrangea, petals pale blue and cool as the skin draped
      over what's left of this flesh. You're either beside me,

Still sleeping and about to wake, or you're not. I don't know,
      and I don't want to. For now, Otis and Isaac, Lou and a fragile
Soprano keep my sad company, but you'll be home soon. I'll drag
      my ass into the kitchen, fix us something to eat, and then all evening,
All through the evening, I'll hold you hard to everything that hurts.

The Soul as Perpetually Eighteen Years Old

So suddenly resurgent acne and a stammering speech,
    or else I go full bore and without apparent

Thought, a verbal spiral down to that embarrassed pause
    which all assembled know was never meant to end

A sentence but simply must, must, like that old circling
    into the self and each little thing—glance from woman,

Sun on face—held so dear, so long, the whole damn system
    collapses of its own weight, and then, cyst come

To a head or dying star, critical mass, can no longer contain
    itself so that all I can see is the pain I imagine

Every other living creature suffers, pain like a rock
    on the back or else that miniaturized version

Of the OED, which, when you hold at last the magnifier
    above the page you see is nothing but an exhaustive

Etymology, glyph to rune to the Roman alphabet's
    loving serifs, of *great sorrow,* its derivatives from *you*

And *I* to *country, people,* and the unspeakable things
    we call God while we stare in the mirror, drunk

And alone late some Saturday night, while we question
    each last thing we were told, *salvation* and *grace,*

Justice and *faith*, what it means *to be given* and what it means
    to earn, and so the things we thought we'd do with

Our lives. Do you see what I mean? So lucky now to be alive.

Permanent Collection

I kept a few things: a cylinder of crimson sealing wax,
    a handful of cut and tumbled and polished stones,

And a custom-made rubber stamp from which rises
    a cracked and ink-stained signature no one

Will ever sign again. I don't know why he needed any of it,
    my grandfather, a man who, so far as I know,

Wore one of two pairs of overalls every day of his life.
    And I don't know why I needed it, though at the time,

Dividing up what remains of a man, it seemed important
    that some things too worthless to even be considered

For sale not be consigned to the eventual archeology
    of the county landfill. What would the future guess

About a man who kept a broken drill bit of every size,
    mason jar lids with spoiled seals, and fifty-gallon drums

Of unsorted rock collected from the continent's western third?
    Even the most generous interpretation seemed

A little inhumane. As if some meaning could be divined
    from this thing or that thing, as if they could be anything

But reminders we only ever half-believe we must go
    from this place, that all our work amounts to nothing

More than an estate sale or a thrift store's jumbled racks.
　　And of course, I'm guilty of the same thing, having placed

These few small keepsakes on a shelf where I'll see them
　　sometimes in passing, where they'll play as lesser figures

In an incomplete mythology I'll build up around them,
　　where they will be still, be dusted. They are

My own unfinished work now, a handful of minor plot points
　　in another volume of a story no one will read. It too

Will gather dust in the Permanent Collection, its call number
　　misfiled, its binding unbroken and unremarkable.

At the front desk, Eternity's librarian is weaving a pencil
　　back and forth through her delicate fingers or building

Little houses of unused sign-out cards. She's not much of a reader,
　　and besides, the books are all the same: false starts

And detail. Each day at the appointed hour, she advances
　　the numbers on her date-stamp, never ceasing

To be amazed at how the little click of time echoes
　　against the lobby's cold and infinitely polished marble.

The Soul as Rooms for Rent

Good light a few hours each morning and cheap,
    just you'll want to think about the neighborhood—

Not dangerous, don't misunderstand—just dead, storefront
    church and hourly-rate motel boarded up both.

Buses don't run past eight and not at all on Sundays.
    Means you've got to think ahead since the market's

Gone under, but honey, you don't look like a big eater,
    and I bet you like quiet some too. We've got that,

Quiet. I'd bet, in fact, this is just the kind of place
    you were hoping for. Over there's the stove—

Pilot's out but it works fine, don't worry—, and that, well,
    that's Formica, not original, but looking out

There's the under-eaves scrollwork, only wanting some paint
    and maybe the thrashers' nests cleared out.

Or maybe not. Nothing here, the hardwood
    sure echoes. That walnut? Maple? Anyway,

I bet you don't have a whole lot of furniture. No.
    This is just the place for you. And we can do

Month-to-month. Whatever you need. I don't know,
    you could set up a little table beneath the window there,

Make yourself a cup of coffee, maybe get some work done.
    Just imagine that. Wouldn't that be lovely?

The Soul as Episode in the Supermarket

It sleeps when the limbs are active.
PINDAR

Always at the worst times, always without warning
   he abandons his studies, his napping, hands pressed

Between thighs, and flutters in the warmth of his perch
   hidden down between the diaphragm and the tightly-packed

Lobes of the abdominal organs he would not deign
   to touch. Up the vena cava and into the chest cavity,

My whole thorax lights up as he climbs rib by burning
   rib. I'm helpless. It's got to be something about the scene

Here at the intersection of *Produce* and a plasticized recreation
   of an idea of a butcher shop that's caught his ever-dilated eye—

So many things from his books—muscle's marbling
   under cling-wrap, speckled cross-section of bone,

Citrus shipped from overseas and piled in fruit carts
   with cardboard wheels, fiber and pith, the stem cell,

The marrow, cilantro and antiseptic, bodies of shoppers
   layer by layer by moistened layer, a place he could hide,

Hum of compressors and a piped-in thunderclap
   as the greens take their mist, pectin, blood, hundreds

Of gallons of water, jugged, and help us he's beginning to sing,
    O abundance, Little Stevie Wonder's silk and tink-

Tink of piano, price per ounce: this is his ascension;
    the recitation of checkers' names, hair colors, ring sizes

Has begun. I try to swallow. He's in the esophagus, a talon lodged
    in the trachea. I grin like an idiot, ready to buckle at the knees.

Apocalypse When?

So this is how it ends: kettle's steam and piercing whistle,
    the freshly broken seal on a carton of oats;
Then, just as the mug's burning brim's brought to the lips,

    it's the radio news announcer, clear as any black herald's call:
Twenty-seven minutes to The Hour. But what sort of reckoning
    is this? April morning, slight hangover, jays strafing,

One last time, the dog in the unmown yard. Sure, in hindsight,
    there was the plague's sea of fly-specked orphans,
Trails of dead endless in every direction, whole continents

    turned the color of sand. But it was all so distant, and the other signs
Amounted to what? A few more scattered missing persons
    for the rapture's great bellwether and police still without a clue?

Another glass-eyed and lifeless wave of fish on the lakeshore,
    crows gulping down flesh like there's no tomorrow?
And as always, it's not till later, much later, after those final minutes

    and the ridiculous question of what to do with them—settling,
Finally, on oats and coffee and radio news—that the whole story
    becomes clearer, though still it's buried on page A22 and lacking

A byline: *Senators Filibuster in Lowest Chamber of Hell.* The debate,
    it seems, has been going on for ages, and this is nothing
But the latest default extension of current laissez-faire policies

until some solution's found for this wholly unprecedented flood
Of immigrants anticipated from above. Some call for containment:
a wall constructed from the surplus femurs of children honed

To a razor's edge, a moat of serpent infested and boiling blood.
Others push for a limited-integration jobs program, work that's done
Out of sight. The furnaces, after all, must be stoked, and someone's

got to collect the bristles of the Beast so that the organ meats
Of CEOs might be scrubbed raw. But for now, the sticking point's
a simple question of procedure, and, wouldn't you know,

Along with the other books, *Robert's Rules of Order* has been burned.
This could take eternities, and so blood runs through some streets
While twilight glints on the freshly poured asphalt of others. Below,

they're screeching still. Tell me, just tell me, what's a lost soul to do?

Inner City Circular Saw Cosmology Blues

The only one who hasn't punched out a little early, he shudders
    fifteen half-constructed stories above the city, which seems

Holy, a moment, in its silence until he realizes the six lanes
    of bumper-to-bumper nothingness below exhale a haze

Of diesel and ozone and tar strong enough
    to choke the grace out of anything. He can believe

In hell—he knows it to the lowest levels of the car-park—
    but heaven, that's an idea no venture capitalist would touch;

God would never make it past the receptionist's worldly eye,
    denied admittance for His trembling, unmanicured hands,

His wrinkled project proposal. But heaven or no, there's work
    to be done before he descends; he runs the day's final cut,

And as the blade spins down it settles into a contralto's
    sweetest note. He can hardly believe a sound so pure

Could rise from a machine so brutal, so inexact, as if instead
    an angel, dingy in its gown, had laid an empty hat

In the sanctified dust and started its song for the skeletal
    frame of a bankrupt, unfinishable paradise behind it.

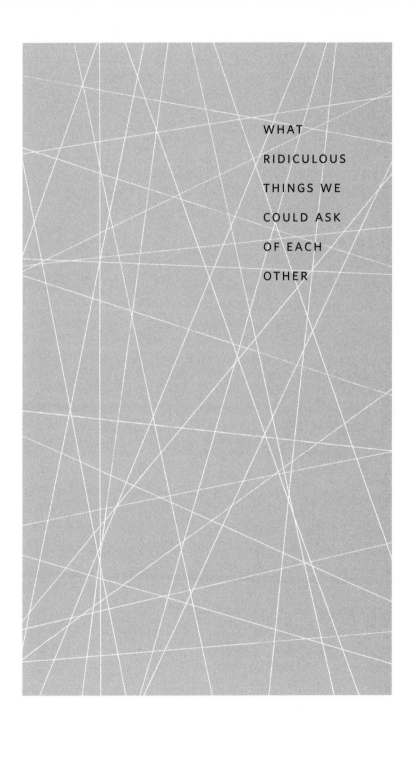

WHAT
RIDICULOUS
THINGS WE
COULD ASK
OF EACH
OTHER

To the Unexploded H-Bomb Lost in Tidal Mud
off the Coast of Savannah, Georgia

Forehead blotch and breadlines on the little black-and-white's
   nightly news, the thing was half-decayed by the time
I knew it was there, some background noise while we ate

   meat loaf around the kitchen table's laminate, reassured
By the stable sheen of Reagan's hair, the small humor of his small
   jokes. Why worry? No duck and cover, no bomb shelter's hatch

Behind pyracanthas, just waxwings' slick camo, their breasts
   the dust color of the few remaining air-raid sirens
Scattered around the old parts of town and so long silent

   I had to ask, finally, what they were. When my father
Got to the core of it—*from each according to his ability, to each*
   according to his need—, I couldn't understand the problem.

What did I know? What do I? You'll outlive me and each of us,
   chances are, or else we'll go all at once. Thing that worries me
Is your patience. You spin off a neutron here and there

   while I fool myself into thinking there might be some future
In this; even today, dead of winter's sudden thaw, sun and some color
   once again in the world, I crossed the quad out front of the library,

Wind cracking the flag like a whip, and the masses' quick
   every-which-way fused, a flock at some common task.
The waxwing's a bird that'll pass a berry to its neighbor: *friend, eat—*

only after you—please, friend, I insist. Caught up in sudden hope
I'll believe anything. That one more miserable and poorly dressed
    cohort of grad students staring at the tarnished floors of third-story

Efficiencies and still not reading the evening's stack of articles
    would, were they sober, were they not trying to hear something
Beyond the silence their lives had unexpectedly become,

    be enough to save us, that their collective good works
Might amount to more than uncalled call numbers or a thumb-smudge's
    tarnish against the radiance of the sovereign's weekend belt-buckle.

You, you'd like the way he swaggers with it: blunt force,
    high yield, dumb culmination of history's wrongs.
And how can I argue with that, uncertain even of this moment's

    potential? One suspect move and they'll all scatter.
I look for a sign, listen, and if there's anything behind the random
    click and scuff of footsteps on concrete, it's you,

The Geiger-crackle of what will not step back from the brink.

The Soul as Kaczynski

It reveals a judgment . . . of woe drawing nigh.

PINDAR

He looks like hell. And with the first hint of daybreak's
 tobacco stain beyond the trees, haze-obscured

As if by floods of dust picked up in rotor-wash at Kirkuk,
 at San Sebastián, at Dealey Plaza, he surveys the devastation

Of his face in a small mirror and begins a litany
 against the unreal: *That I have suffered the punch card,*

The modem, Ma Bell, have suffered TV news, flyovers,
 and at the hands and boots of the U.S. Marshal, on the table

Pipe, powder, a handful of matches from which he proceeds
 to snip, one by one, the heads with a pair of wire cutters,

Text message and cell phones' chirp and rattle, iPod, ATMs' questions
 and the bright tones of their synthesized speech no matter the hour,

The mood, and how much I might want to be left, simply, alone
 with the rain-swollen particleboard which litters the curbside,

Carefully, it must be done with great care, he seals
 the pipe, sun's light incendiary now through the window,

Purposelessness, Irish Pubs in airports at Atlanta, Dubai, Detroit,
 that I've suffered cheap veneer and the Nothing everyone else has refused,

The trigger's beautiful and simple: rubber band's
    tension, fence nail, then the match heads' quick sulfur and

Saint Ludd, Holy Martyrs of the Haymarket, Saint Emiliano Zapata,
    bless the bird and the rain and what will be the ruins

Of cities, bless the market crashed and walking in peace,
    bless legions of honeybees even as they fall from the sky,

And so let the postmark secure the path of its own undoing,
    let the money, the memo, let each hard drive wired in sequence

Burn; let us forget everything. Trompe l'oeil? Blow it up.
    Bless what we knew before we knew so much, before that freedom,

And bless, before everything, fire.

J. Steals from the Rich and Uses the Money to Get Drunk Again

> Only those of us who carry our cause in our hearts are willing to run the risks.
>
> RIGOBERTA MENCHÚ

Too much to lose, he thinks, for anything else, picking pockets,
    say, casually, without arousing suspicion out front of downtown's
Banks and boutiques where late-afternoon yellows shop-windows,
    yellows this gabardine's hushed protest as one more wallet's lifted,
Palmed, and repocketed in the darkness of a credit score's grave.
    Another round on me echoes as the first handful of earth drops
Without ceremony on the casket's lid. Just too much at stake
    for anything so romantic, so this: the legal, if not entirely ethical
Raid on their children's college funds. In truth, he barely skims
    the top. An adjunct's wage. Nothing, really. Still, the students,
Over half of whom this semester are majoring in Business
    Administration, hardly get what the parents pay for.
They ought to be learning something useful, how, for instance,
    to begin without the slightest pang of guilt yet another memo
Which though one could never know it by reading the thing
    will mean the disappearance of another thousand jobs, workers
Waking to confusion one morning as the sun reveals nothing
    where, once, a livelihood had been. Instead, empty parking lots,
Temporary fencing. How will these kids ever learn the dead
    and bureaucratic English in which inevitably the worst of news
Is delivered when he's leading again what may someday become
    a discussion on civil disobedience? How can they hope to master
Those conjugations and suffixes which most effectively liquidate
    blame, responsibility, when he keeps count of third-world states

Toppled this week alone in foreign-backed military coups?
He should be precise, teach the five-paragraph essay's perfect
Compartmentalization, its solid structural apparatus capable
of pacifying any guerrilla conscience, any full accounting
Of an argument's collateral effects. Twelve hundred words, please,
on a streamlined workforce and profit maximization. Don't forget
The bibliography. Too much to lose then for anything much beyond
debating whether to add his name to another online petition,
An act too likely already to get a person placed on a watch-list.
He couldn't stand a night in jail even for those things he does
Believe. So nothing: afterwork afternoon buried in Happy Hour's
mass grave, the hinge of his briefcase's shoulder strap adds
A cricket's chirp to his cadence. He walks to the bus, imagines
the stand of trees wherein the revolution must be gathering.
All the way home, he practices. He's learning Spanish
and just drunk enough not to care what the other riders
Think of this crazy book-bagged and brown-blazered white boy
as he mouths the words along with the voice in his headphones.
No, not *white boy*. *Gringo*, he thinks, his lips parting to the useless
yellowing expanse of his vocabulary: *libre, liberar, libertad.*

J. Listens to Line Static on the Last Pay Phone
in the Continental U.S.

Constant as motion, constant as noise had become, bus ride
  and transfer and bus ride, commuters' headphones' thudding bass
And the rhythmless bleeps of text-messaging, it made no sense,
  the city still, so completely near silence. Hum of something
Distant, faint sizzle of static on the line, the phone's smudged chrome
  reflecting without precision twilight's thin and oily slick
On wet pavement, the crackle, here and there, of road salt
  as he shifts his weight. The truth of the matter's clear enough.
No dial tone, no operator: disconnected. And what then,
  the receiver placed back into the cradle of outdated technology?
Not long, even the coin return'll be bricked up; one more final thing
  will be gone. What won't soon succumb? A few blocks
And a hundred miles of unlit neon down, the last polar bear,
  having lost it all in the long and continuing recession of ice,
Is out on a bender with the single remaining due-paying member
  of the United Auto Workers. Days they wallow: recall the hunt,
Describe the operation of the punch press; nights: the bar
  until closing. They tell each other jokes, the laugh line
Always the same: *You're killing me.* Everyone else wishes
  they'd get out, but what is there for them? Nostalgia
Can't keep the furnace lit and two don't make much
  of a picket line. Finally, it can't be anything but the wind's hiss,
Its smell of stray dogs' teeth, house fires still snapping,
  smoldering, or else in full bloom, the mayor's breath.
He's giving a speech before the Council: *Look,* he says, members
  of the Chamber of Commerce's eyes glazed over as they imagine

The whole emaciated length of the body politic, how they might
    portion what remains between them, fingers, friction, thigh,
At all we've done. Pay phone and corner store, foot traffic, the sidewalk
    itself. To be razed then, by time alone, mortar's inability,
Winter after winter, to keep from crumbling? To be deemed
    obsolete, unnecessary, to be condemned, marked officially,
To wait, then, as if without end? All I hear is the groan of buildings
    held together by nothing more than the flourish of a spray can
And smoke damage's matte undercoat. In their bunkers
    redevelopers huddle round their project proposals, new
Hotel-casinos along the riverfront, the little balsa models
    complete with blond and brief-cased citizens heading briskly
Towards what? A symposium on White Flight & the Gentrification
    of Rust? The microphone bleeds feedback all through the empty
Panel discussion. The afterparty reeks of asbestos and lead.
    I want to believe, I really do, that what in me and each one of us
Is good-for-nothing, because it cannot feed itself, because it cannot
    pay for food or, therefore, a phone small enough to embed
In its fingernail is not better off abandoned in the dumpster
    behind the vacant metaphysician's office among a few minor gods'
Withered husks and carbon copies of old invoices. Elegy
    is stupid, if you can avoid it. And if the whole bright blueprint
Of human history from tabula rasa to city on the hill adds up
    to nothing but a canceled bus-route, another scraping to ground?
To see what I can't imagine, something not already plotted in blood
    or etched in bone or prophesied in the grid behind a subdivision's
Thick gates. But who can see anything in this failing light? Hell,
    from this far off, the pillar of ash may as well be a granite column.

J. Resists the Urge to Comment on Your Blog

> Birds appear to be singing at night to avoid competition with the
> high noise levels caused by our cities during the day.
>
> BBC NEWS

Above the eight-lane's unexpected bottlenecks, brake lights'
    red clogging the hardened arteries of commerce,
Dawn's gone slack again in the sky's early sulfur, the lusterless
    leaves of oleanders, the few stark and persisting eucalyptus
In which mockingbirds dismantle beetles, dilate and constrict
    their irises' brimstone, wait for The Hour to come.
We can't fault them for not trying. They gave an honest shot at
    competition: studied the form of the personalized ring tone,
Learned the car alarm's frantic medley. But a few smog-dulled
    and twittering birds up against our great monopoly
Of noise? Good luck. Each as yet undelivered bill's glassine
    crinkles in the mail-carrier's bag; each wireless headset
Is set to voice-activated. The problem's basic economics:
    cheap goods. A glut on the market. The radio buzzes.
Infrastructure creaks out neglect's old tune, which, since it offers
    nothing for sale, no one can hear anyway. And now someone's
Gone and stuck a sheet of vellum between us and the sky.
    Light aches, and here, morning coffee and laptop, I'm already
Just one all-too-clever screen name from telling that blunt
    anonymity we once thought of as the vast and numinous world
To go fuck itself. It's hard to even imagine what that means,
    harder still to find a moment for imagining the bus-stop
Amputees, the grandmothers, the data-entry experts writhing
    with the pain of their lower backs, the motorists' eyes, all

Sparrow-jittery as they try to guess which adjacent truck's
      a thermonuclear bomb in disguise, which lane change
Might best position them upwind of fallout, how to hold
      the ever-present Other at bay. And to imagine then
How my easy curse obliterates them, how, even before that,
      my thinking of them at all cements their ankles in abstraction
At the end of The Real's pier. Waves lap at the pilings.
      Another day drifts off in the ocean of the CPU fan's hum.
And what about you, little aparatchik? What's your status
      update? How many sit-ups, how many hours at the treadmill
Till you achieve something remotely like your online avatar's
      sleek coding? I'm sorry, what was it you asked? Something
About The Self? What an awful racket it makes! Data clacking
      as we hoist it around, all that weight which is not us but rather
Some romanticization or obfuscation or the details of a story
      we'd like to imagine we've a part in. It got to the point I thought
The mockers were on to something, mockery now such common
      currency, in their silence. So what, a general strike? An embargo
Against what's not humane? A little *good luck* chirrups down
      from the eaves. But it's no good. I end up talking
With you when you're not here and forgetting to fill you in
      on the details of our conversation. I was thinking of what,
When we take away what obscures, is left there. Latitude
      and longitude. Height, weight, and hair color. The way I thought
Of sending you something, a small gift or note, how I've retreated
      so far into my own void that thought became real as anything
And so got you nothing and left me with one more half-remembered
      non-event. Look, somewhere a mist's just beginning to lift;
Somewhere ice ratchets away from other ice and slips into the sea.
      This city's stucco's started to flake; the bare, blank substrate's
Looking right at us. Feeling is something's going to give,
      and we've got to be ready, you and I. In shadow inscribe

Sycamores' bark with shadow; in end of day's color-leeched light
  leave bougainvillea, leave hibiscus. On retaining walls, graffiti's
Bright apocalypse; on security's *Armed Response* sign, *Eat the Rich.*
  In silence begin our campaign of whispers, our campaign of sighs.
Black-market speech. The good stuff. What we say'll make flesh
  feel like flesh again, make the blood in the bones itch to get out,
Set skin taut as the wire from which now little bursts of song fire,
  guiding, covertly, our way. Just remember, it's not safe out there.
Guard jealously your thumb's ridges and whorls, your irises' nebulae.
  We've got to go quietly; Love, we move under cover of dark.

J. Finds in His Pocket Neither Change nor Small Bills

Griffith Park, Los Angeles

Every living heart ... all over this broad land, will yet swell ..., when again
touched, as surely they will be, by the better angels of our nature.
ABRAHAM LINCOLN

Because the body now and its organs suggest nothing
     but those pathologies in which we've been instructed,
Because the gutter's black as new blood, a Petri dish
     of piss and teeth knocked loose at the root,
Because our walking here's scared up pigeons and the air's
     thick with their disease, because, therefore, we're holding
Our breath in silent prayer, Good People of Los Angeles,
     for our immune systems, for hand sanitizer,
For swift and decisive return of the sun's irradiating
     grace, I can hardly say I even know you much
Beyond the turnstile's slick in the discount supermarket,
     the sidewalk's chewing gum and tuberculosis.
But I've been thinking of you, of your eyes darting behind
     the tinted lenses which minimize exposure to UV, to God-
Knows-what, even though it's dark this morning, cold, cold,
     at least, by our way of thinking: frond-tips glimpsed
Through fog-bank, a dew so lightly acidic we've forgotten
     it's the cause of these few more leaves dropped
From evergreens, the rasp at the back of the throat.
     Members of the Taxpayer's Association, divorce
Attorneys, Good People of Bel-Air, you who keep eyes dead-
     ahead at the top of freeway off-ramps, who refuse guilt,

That scrap cardboard *hungry* sign slung over a stack of bones,
    entrance within the Town Car's four doors, the pure, leather-
Scented air there, I've been thinking about those
    other ones, the thousands of indigents and itinerants,
Formerly among us and suffering the debit card's curse
    on the panhandler, who today, because it is December
And dark, because after cremation they've gone so long
    unclaimed, will be buried in mass anonymity somewhere
Far from here, Boyle Heights or East L.A., somewhere
    unremarkable: flatland, barred windows, chain-link.
There's a minimum of ceremony. A short benediction
    and half a handful of city employees. Dogs watch
From a distance. It takes a certain kind of distraction,
    a remarkable forgetfulness to not recognize
In those nameless something of that little tyrant, The Self,
    to let history and language fail, let the world outside
Dissolve, a mentholated lozenge on the tongue.
    The taste it leaves is the inability to taste anything else,
And at bottom of the park's southern slope, beneath
    the Hollywood Hills and their Attendant, Contempt, one
Who's wandered a few too many blocks from the halfway
    house's steadying three-times-daily belts into Los Feliz
Boulevard's early rush a few bars of *O Lord,*
    won't you buy me a Mercedes Benz? before schizophrenia
Changes key again into abject terror's primal screech.
    What's remarkable then is the passing jogger's scandalized
I could just die and the morning's usual by-the-numbers.
    All over the basin psychotherapists await the DSM-V's
New-phone-book thud on the doorstep, and grave-shift
    cryogenicists make the last rounds, check temps, check
The corresponding boxes on log sheets while we continue
    in our unrelenting interrogation of the body: *Liver!*

How do you plot against me today? Brain! You've gone soft. As if
     deep-within's crowded tissues could confess the knowledge
We most desire, as if we'd not already allowed our private
     pandemic to order our days as on a clear plastic pill case,
As if, I mean, *to function* were synonymous with *to live.*
     Right down to it, we all know Death's no more likely
To knock and announce than the LAPD, and though
     he may be gentler, he will not, in the end, read perfunctorily
From a list of rights meant to protect us. Everything
     we've said has always been used against us. *Los Feliz*:
The Happy Ones. We mispronounce. Force a rhyme
     with *Felix*. Mispronounce and counteract even irony's
Potential side effects. *Los Feliz. The Homeless. The Lesser
     and Underprivileged. The Disturbed. May they all someday
Rest in peace. Good night, Sweet Paupers.* Abstraction's
     its own little crime against humanity, but *euphemism*
Is still a lovely word to say aloud. *Los Ángeles.*
     But what angel is this? Stretched half across the footpath,
Its body's a grotesque, everywhere swollen
     and withered at once. It's gone septic; it's gone
Almost entirely. And what worthless paper is that man
     fumbling with as he approaches? A thinning five maybe,
Lincoln's etched face a gaunt pockmark, beard and ears,
     or else the "Elegy for Sky & Gooseflesh" penciled
On an expired bus transfer? It's a worthless scene:
     a man in headphones and an angel which actually appears
To be something much more like a beggar, except
     that it's passed out and so freed of the beggar's contractual
Obligations. Starved and curled into itself, it looks
     freed even of this world, like something almost not
There at all, a fact the man uses as excuse to keep walking,
     his step timed to the beat, his eyes scanning ahead

For needles, slivered glass, the more subtle sort of dangers.
 What else could he possibly do? Kneel down
And slip stealthily something into the blistered palm
 of its hand? Cover its body with the fallen fronds
Which we can't now help but imagine as resembling wings
 because we're thinking instead of a man slowly dying
In a public park about a real angel and so The Eternal
 and so the failing health of our own souls, a disorder
For which the FDA has yet approved no treatment? *Disorder*,
 as if it were simply a matter of finding the right arrangement
Of bodies in space. But what can we do, all exactly mad
 with grief for ourselves or hobbled with debt's deep-
Tissue bruise? Because in mourning we are to gather
 together, Shoppers of the Miracle Mile, Day Traders,
Night Watchmen, but we're all just standing here
 like fools, unable to look each other in the eyes,
Unable to believe in anything at the unchanging core
 of being but a phantom limb's complete and constant
Wing-ache, because we are what multiplies, the desert
 as it reaches towards even you, Citizens of the Once Frozen
North. In mourning we are to remember, but memory's
 emaciated; there was something supposed to become *more*
Perfect, something else about what always comes of tyrants,
 but who knows? In mourning we meet in need,
But here in a circle at last, tell me what ridiculous things
 we could possibly ask of each other. Spare a buck?
Sing a little prayer for me? The overcast buckles
 under the weight of a singed and empty sky. Because
There's next to nothing left, America, call our
 name; please, won't you please lay on your hands?

Notes

"J. Learns the Difference between Poverty and Having No Money"—
While Ernesto Trejo's "E" poems serve as inspiration for the whole "J"
series, this poem also owes an image to Trejo's "Entering a Life."

"Early Service at the Temple of Angelino Heights"—For William Archila
and Lory Bedikian

"The Soul as a Kind of Life I Sort of Lived Once"—979 Ferry Ln. #6,
Eugene, Oregon.

"Old News and the Borrowed Blues"—Epigraph from *Relaxing with the
Miles Davis Quintet*, track one

"The Soul as Perpetually Eighteen Years Old"—Thanks to Carlos Ramírez

"To the Unexploded H-Bomb Lost in Tidal Mud off the Coast of
Savannah, Georgia"—On February 5, 1958, a B-47 collided in midair with
an F-86 during the course of training exercises. Damaged, the B-47 was
forced to jettison the MK-15 hydrogen bomb it was carrying. It has not
been found.

"The Soul as Kaczynski"—Theodore Kaczynski, the neo-Luddite
"Unabomber"

"J. Steals from the Rich and Uses the Money to Get Drunk Again"—
Epigraph from *I, Rigoberta Menchú*; this poem is for all of my wonderful
students, especially Hillary, Aaron, Alana, Rachel, Anna, Jordan, Craig,
and George.

"J. Listens to Line Static on the Last Pay Phone in the Continental U.S."—
The Latin in the epigraph translates as "We Hope for Better Things; It
Shall Rise from the Ashes." Detroit adopted this motto after an 1805 fire
devastated it.

"J. Finds in His Pocket Neither Change nor Small Bills"—Epigraph from
Lincoln's first inaugural